SYSTEM TO IMPROVE MONETARLY.

FIRST EPISODE.

PREAMBLE.

To begin with, let me tell you that there is a precept of success and economic improvement. People, if they propose it, can get to know, and use this system without any doubt. It is clear that there are many people who do not know this system, the reason is because this system is hidden from our senses, and our capacity for perception, with which, in the first instance, it could seem sub realistic, however, never again. far from reality.

The reason why we have not assimilated it through those people who do use it is because those same people who are successful are not aware that they are applying it, in

A certain period of time, they are using it without really knowing what they are doing.

But there is nothing extraordinary about all this. I have understood this system in the most valuable, and special, of all the books that exist today. I confirm that this system of economic improvement has a sustainable basis, because the mere fact of commenting on it is not enough to assimilate it. Much more is needed than just commenting on this system, it is necessary to deeply meditate on the content that is exposed in this book, to get to assimilate what is being transmitted here.

However, this system is a great opportunity that can give you the opportunity to improve financially.

Some time ago, I met a person who used this system, and managed to succeed in life repeatedly. For my part, I wish you with all my heart, that you achieve your goals

Economical. Your social status, your condition, etc., etc., are really not relevant. With this system you can obtain results, as long as what is stated here is applied correctly.

In other words, if you have a minimum of economy, you will be able to make an exchange of this good, for some benefit such as; The one that your hairdresser, carpenter, plumber, etc., etc. lends you, where I want to go with all this, is that in the civilized life that we have lived, it is sustained with transactions, the provision of assistance in exchange for a benefit.

It is clear that if you want, you can offer some kind of benefit to someone special, and without expecting anything in return, no benefit, no favor, or profit. Over time, you will realize that it is very unlikely to live with other people, without obtaining some type of benefit. We are conditioned

Make exchanges of a benefit for a benefit.

I think that all the people who read this book, may be interested enough to assimilate the first lesson of the economic improvement system. I have stumbled upon this system many times, for quite some time, long before I could come to understand this system. In the Bible, this system reflects it this way:

THE ONE WHO WANTS TO BECOME GREAT AMONG YOU, BE YOUR SERVANT AND THE ONE WHO WANTS TO BE THE FIRST AMONG YOU, BE YOUR SERVANT "mat. 19, 26-27 ".

I came to understand that this does not mean that I had to quit my job, to become a lackey. Most likely, he would have been a lackey without much motivation. It is clear that it would be preferable for me to achieve positive achievements through my own profession. This is the true meaning.

LESSON ONE OF THE ECONOMIC IMPROVEMENT SYSTEM.

(THAT THE ONE AMONG YOU WHO IS GREAT BE ALLOWED TO TAKE CARE OF THE NEEDS OF THE PEOPLE; THAT THE ONE AMONG YOU WHO IS A CHIEF MAY SERVE, ACCORDING TO THEIR CAPACITIES).

This system is currently incomplete. It is only the first lesson. Besides, you don't have to take it as it comes.

It is obvious that the great characters triumphed by attending to what the people need, such as: Archimedes, Albert Einstein, etc., etc.,

The truth is that inventions such as the printing press, with it culture and information, became popular and reached the whole world. It was invented by Johannes Gutenberg in 1400, and a hundred years later it was working all over Europe on a massive scale. Gutenberg would thus become one of the

Most famous and influential inventors in the history of mankind, because the printing press produced an indisputable impact on the dissemination of information and, therefore, the democratization of education, in this way by worrying about meeting a certain need of the people , managed to become an important person. This same circumstance has been repeated throughout history with other inventors, the same happens with businessmen, entrepreneurs, writers, etc., etc., their contribution is the equivalent of the amount of population whose needs are attended to. In 1903, the Wright brothers fulfilled one of human dreams: flying, but not only did they meet the needs of the people around them, they also met the needs of more generations.

Therefore, some of us who are bosses without becoming very important people, having achieved some success, have managed to become what they are, attending

In accordance with their capabilities, without taking advantage of a large mass of the population, because they serve a limited number of people, a reduced sector of people, and this can be applied with businessmen, artists, entrepreneurs, etc., etc. ., this is extended to all those people who have liberal professions. His triumph, however moderate it may be, is due to the benefits in the context of his ability, or specialization. Many times they will not become famous, but will stand out from the great mass of the population.

The servant only serves a few people, yet the successful entrepreneur serves a large mass of people. As a result, the last example serves more people more, and achieves greater results than the first example.

In this case he pays attention, how is it possible that there are many people who work hard to meet the needs of their peers, and

Are they not successful in their projects? How is it possible that other people who get jobs of a certain responsibility, and at a certain moment find themselves in oblivion again? These questions will not be answered by this lesson. I know more lessons are needed that will be explained as this book is read. However, you have already understood the following:

THIS FIRST LESSON, DESPITE NOT BEING A BROKEN RULE OF TRIUMPH, IS A PRECEPT THAT MUST BE KEPT, TO OBTAIN, AND GET PROFITS.

Look closely at the word (DESERVE). Is there undeserved success ?. Unfairly, yes. This triumph has not been the result of the efforts made, rather because of the damages that other people have suffered as a result of certain arts promoted to the latter. Currently, one of the problems that

Unfortunately, nations have it, it is caused by some men who make great fortunes, therefore "success is no longer a correct term" following this line. An example, the result obtained from a bet made by a player, comes from the losses of another player. Now it is no longer an exchange of a provision of a service for an economic good.

The great masses of money that, for example, are obtained in the city of skyscrapers New York, obtained by investment operations in a short time, is usually the result of the accumulation of losses that thousands and thousands of small investors have suffered. Large bags of money obtained in this way would not be admissible. Of course, if these small investors didn't bother to act in the same way, I mean, get a lot of money as a result of causing losses to their fellows, rather than offering them a good service as a fair exchange. Anyway, there is

It should be pointed out that long-term investment is a benefit that is offered to a community, because it offers useful means for development.

There are other ways of exchanging in a short space of time, on investment platforms, or in everyday life, which only produce profits for the losses suffered by other people. If the opportunity presented itself to me, I would not help someone to break this law of life.

At this time we can analyze the second precept of the Mystic Law regarding wealth and success. I have found in the Bible a couple of commandments that are considered the compilation of all the laws and prophecies. The first is not in the context of this book, the second informs us: (Love your neighbor as yourself). Many people understand with this that we have to approve formal feelings with our peers, a positive feeling in the internal forum

From ourselves, an incentive to improve our emotions, in a similar way to that experienced when contemplating a newborn baby. A posteriori I understood that I was wrong.

Is it possible to compare what a mother feels for her child with another feeling of affection? No, since it would be like comparing a truly profound feeling with another more superficial feeling, one feeling is more cordial for temporary situations, and the other is deeper, where there is no objection when giving everything for his offspring , even if it cost your health or well-being. One is rather a benefit that we give ourselves, the other is valid to fulfill an end that is to give everything unconditionally, from a truly deep and pure feeling. This positive feeling in rather an imagination, only when it comes from a service, and only in this way, is it dealing with love. Is the human being of good

Corazon is satisfied in putting a good face on another person with serious problems, and then continues on his way as if nothing had happened. No, they stop to offer some kind of help or service, love without a benefit is not love, a benefit is its measure. Ways of thinking like this have led me to understand the real feeling of this commandment.

SECOND LESSON OF THE ECONOMIC
IMPROVEMENT SYSTEM.

(SERVE YOUR NEIGHBOR AS YOURSELF)

Some reader of this book will think: "heck this is
just philanthropy, in this way no one can become
a millionaire." On the contrary, power can and
has been achieved. I want Gutemberg to forgive
me, since I am going to mention it again, because
I prefer to comment on examples that we already
know, and it can help us to understand things.
Did he serve his fellow men as he would have
done for himself? I believe that at that time this
Lord would think, if I were an economically
average man, what kind of information would I
like to have? How could I obtain it? How could it
help me? How regularly could it be on sale? And
then I build the first printing press, providing a
service, as he would have liked it to have been
provided.

Only a person with a passion for the provision of a service would have in his mind that any of his readers after finishing reading a copy of one of his newspapers, would be left with the feeling of looking forward to the next publication, to go buy another copy, since the newspaper you have just read has met all your expectations, and you have the feeling of wanting more of the same.

The fact that Gutemberg wanted to provide a service to his community, offering the type of information that he would have liked to have been offered, in a constant and regular way, with an avant-garde methodology, for that time, leaving the information printed , thus avoiding forgetting in time, that he got a great surprise in the collection of the services that he had offered to his community, a surprise that over time led to a demand from more users of this type of

Service. This type of results is the reward for the provision of a service performed to others, as if you would have liked it to have been done to you.

In any town, make a comparison with the most prosperous entrepreneurs, with their adversaries who have failed their companies, or who remain in business with great difficulty. The triumph implies a high perception of the provision of services, a varied gender carefully supervised, highly qualified employees, in an exquisite environment, and carefully cared for, where the customer feels like someone special, and appreciated, products of the best quality possible. This is the kind of deal that any entrepreneur would like to be offered, if instead of being an entrepreneur he were a client, and yet he is providing it to his users. This merchant cares more about quality, and functionality, than price, chooses an honest price, instead of taking the risk to

Losing results, therefore, this is how you serve and treat your customers.

However, the other side of the coin, we have the one who is on the verge of bankruptcy, who behaves in a way contrary to the previous example. He is in possession of a less diverse warehouse, composed of poor quality items, with which he teases his customers, indoctrinates his customers with bad arts, giving rise to the picaresque, his philosophy for his dissatisfied users, it is full of usury, and little empathy. It is possible that the amount of some of its articles, or services are cheap, or reasonable, but it abuses with the exaggerated price of other articles whose quality is perhaps somewhat questionable.

Since this merchant does not provide his services to his clients, as he would like to be offered, his trade continues on the brink of bankruptcy month after month, or the day of total bankruptcy arrives. It is clear that this merchant does not

He has had prestige. Of course, he can obtain profits outside of this trade, causing economic losses to his clients, with the little recommended system that has just been cited above, he can also cause losses to his suppliers, always sweeping for his own interests. Whoever succeeds by causing damage to others cannot hope to achieve a true victory, regardless of the capital available in the bank.

It should not be said that the success of a high-end store, as I have previously reported, has to be the only way there is, following this route. It is possible that another entrepreneur has the same triumph, or perhaps more, bypassing all the advice I have quoted above. It could be that he devotes himself to the provision of his simplest clients, reducing global expenses to the maximum expression, selling only very cheap items, obtaining a surplus

Quite diminished. This type of service provision can also be qualified as honest, which he would like to receive if he were in the place of his Users. This merchant also applies this second lesson, and succeeds in doing so, despite the fact that his store has a very different image compared to the other store, where every last detail had been carefully cared for, seeing these two types of stores in perspective. They are both applying this same lesson, which I will quote for a better understanding:

(CHOOSE THE CUSTOMER YOU INTEND TO SERVICE, AND SERVE IT HOW YOU WOULD LIKE TO BE SERVED FOR YOU, IF THEY ARE IN THAT SITUATION).

Now you can tell me that the vast majority of people would like to be offered different services in exchange for nothing, without any economic exchange as payment for the merchant. Any entrepreneur who entered

In this situation, he would have to close his business within a few months of lending himself to this situation, thus depriving himself of the probability of offering more services. None of us would be in a privileged situation if he had to be served by merchants who do not exist. The exchanges are of vital importance for today's life. Provision of a service in exchange for financial compensation, in any case, money is a debit or credit service. There is no human being of any gender with a sufficiently well furnished head, who expects to receive some benefit for nothing, unless it is out of compassion, gratitude, mere altruism, etc., which is compensated by the benefit of another. If there were no compensation, there would be no philanthropy either.

It does not take you to be an entrepreneur, or a merchant, to realize the lessons described above. Since these can be applied to any type of activity. A factory salesperson serves its users in the same way

That he does it to his superiors. He also lends himself to attending to the needs of his entire family. When he uses his own economic capital, he is helping all those people who depend on the expenses he makes, such as: pharmacy salesman, tobacconist, coupon salesman, mechanic, watchmaker, shoemaker, etc., etc., motivating in this way to work, contributing to a good environment in their home, teaching their offspring.

If the provision of a service does not attract success, then what is needed? In the first instance, efficiency is needed, efficiency in the provision of any service. This confirmation may seem superficial. The truth is that most of the words that refer to sacred texts, and mystical precepts of existence are stereotypes, because they cannot be avoided. Sooner or later, you will have to face these precepts at some point in your existence.

LESSON THREE OF THE ECONOMIC IMPROVEMENT SYSTEM.

(IT WILL BE GIVEN TO THOSE WHO ARE COMPETENT. THEY WILL HAVE WEALTH. HOWEVER, THOSE WHO ARE NOT COMPETENT WILL LOSE THEIR SKILLS AND MONEY).

This lesson has caused some setbacks. Most of the people who read this book will surely understand what it is about. The absence of rivalry leads to scarcity, at least in the long run.

Have you found someone who has succeeded at some point in his life, without being efficient in his profession or business? (I make an authentic victory here, not to those who earn a lot of money dedicating themselves to trafficking drugs, at the cost of seriously damaging the health of their fellow men).

Many people will mistakenly think that efficiency is just about wisdom or seniority.

Also for some time wisdom was thought to be power. People who have not had any training, no instruction, believe that efficiency is out of hand. However, there are many people who, despite having obtained some training or tutorial above the average, do not show that they are very efficient people. In other words, life is awash with well-trained mediocre graduates. With which, efficiency is not just a matter of study, but rather of committing to doing what one commits to, with full CONVICTION, putting your SOUL, SPIRIT, giving the best that is within your being.

I invite you to reflect on the following quotes that I have found in the Bible:

(THIRST, DILIGENT WITHOUT LOOSE, FERVOROUS OF SPIRIT) "Rom. 12, 11 ".

(WATCH AND BE FIRM IN THE FAITH, WORKING MANLY AND BEING STRONG)

"I Cor. 16, 13 "

(EVERYTHING YOU DO, DO IT WITH THE HEART, AS OBEYING THE LORD AND NOT MEN) "Col. 3, 23 ".

Such quotes hide a profound message about efficiency. Not only do we have to serve others, if not, everything in which we dedicate ourselves we have to do it with true passion, and conviction, so that our performance is superior. Everything we do we have to do it giving the best that is within ourselves. As if the one we were serving were God our Lord, and not our fellow men. We have to immerse ourselves in a state of full enthusiasm and constant motivation. We must remain with the 5 senses fully awake, to improve ourselves, at the same time that we perfect the benefits of our services. In this way we have to behave, not just for a period

From time to time, or provisionally, we have to commit ourselves to internalize this attitude of always applying it throughout our existence.

I already imagine someone who is reading this book, the face that will have been put on him while he thinks: "I do not fit in with the message that is spread here. I will not be able to maintain the necessary constancy day after day, month after month, year after year ". And to be honest no one can achieve it IF THE LEVEL OF MOTIVATION IS NOT CONSTANTLY FUELED BY A DESIRE TO ACHIEVE GOALS, AND OBJECTIVES AT A COMPLETELY HIGHER LEVEL.

Despite the fact that you are sure that success cannot be achieved by any other route, you will not proceed to commit yourself by applying what is disclosed here, no person will do so, "unless motivated by a desire full of intense and constant fervor ", With which I cannot stop thinking about him, day and night, and when he is not

Thinking about your goals and objectives, you are at work, to achieve your dream, and make it come true. If your motivation is at a higher level, then you will be on the right path to achieve your goals.

Put yourself on the trail of the past of any business that has obtained a fair success, you will observe that, at first, the people who raised it, were committed body and soul, day after day, from sunrise to sunset. His triumph was not only the result of an intelligence, the fervor of a desire full of passion, the excessive motivation to give the best that one carries within oneself, the unconditional love for what one is doing is also part of the equation, Promoting you to give yourself one hundred percent of yourself, with which, a positive part of you will be part of everything that you are creating, and that will be perceived by all those people who carry out any exchange or transaction with you . These emotions have made it possible to

Titanic work. It is not possible to achieve success in life without proper motivation. On the contrary, even though we know what to do, without adequate mental aptitude, we will never achieve it.

At the moment that our motivation is high enough (not only in a banal way, but in a completely intense way, that motivates us in a full way, day after day), we will be in possession of the COMPANY SPIRIT.

We appreciate without being conscious, people who have this aptitude, we believe in our internal forum, that we would like to resemble them, or at least, in some details that we admire. We recognize without major problem that they succeed most of the time. Anyway, it must be added that these everyday thoughts are not entirely correct. These subjects do not have a COMPANY SPIRIT. His constant dedication, and his image

Spirit is not about eagerness. They are trained, sometimes against their will, by thoughts that keep them in incessant behavior. This situation takes us to the next level:

LESSON FOUR ON THE ECONOMIC
IMPROVEMENT SYSTEM.

(NOBODY CAN FORCE HIMSELF TO SUCCESS. YOU
NEED TO TRAIN WITH A DOMINANT, CONSTANT
AND SOLID FEELING, OR EMOTION).

If this overriding ability is lacking, the best
intentions, or the brightest plans, the most
earnest wishes, cannot be realized. Success
comes at a price that is normally very high if
things do not unfold within an environment
motivated by a predominant motivating desire.

It takes many sacrifices, over a long period of
time. We will not obey them easily, unless we are
motivated by an internal force powerful enough,
and with the capacity to last over time.

Some thoughts are the consequence of the
product of our instincts. This is the reason

That they are so powerful. The instincts behind these thoughts is a part of our human biology: THE ENERGY OF THE UNIVERSE.

Our internal emotional forum is quite complex, apart from having many incongruities. Various emotions lead us in many different directions. I am referring to hatred, and love, courage, and fear, honesty, and corruption, constancy, and laziness, righteousness, and pasotism, benevolence, and wickedness, etc., the feelings of different characters motivated by different situations, and many more feelings that it would be difficult to quote them all. There are different types of emotions, which underlie various levels of feelings.

We should not be impressed if there are some people who have the spirit of enterprise. Or that they have the facility to change

Behavioral, imprecise, and lacking in aptitude. With which these different skills can drag us towards different routes, efficiency will be very difficult to achieve. Consult a psychiatrist, and they will inform you that most of the disappointments that exist in society are the result of "emotional conflicts." Conflicts are usually the consequence of inefficiency: When we find ourselves worried, and evil is flooding our being, and inner peace, our capacities automatically diminish.

Therefore, we will pay attention to the way these conflicts participate in our efficiency capacities. We end this episode as follows:

1º A person without efficiency is a subject who lacks any predominant feeling, and that several feelings are in constant disagreement, with which, a subject with aspirations subject to ups and downs

Permanent

2º An efficient person is under the influence of a single emotion, which is so strong that it makes the other emotions insignificant, or they become complementary to the predominant emotion, with which, in other words, several feelings support to an emotion, to direct it to the same end.

SECOND EPISODE.

THREE PRECEPTS OF THE ECONOMIC
IMPROVEMENT SYSTEM.

In the previous episode we have analyzed several important precepts that are usually the beginning of triumph. Understanding them is not enough to be able to adapt them. The simple notion of a predominant sentiment does not always lead to success. How and when can they be achieved? Here is a brief orientation:

1st Choose the predominant emotion that is likely to lead us to victory.

2nd Nourish that emotion constantly.

I think there is only one plausible emotion. If I tell you at this precise moment what it is about, surely you find yourself in disagreement. If I classify the other emotions in the first instance, placing on the table the

Complications, and problems that they entail, you will immediately understand that the emotion you have selected is the only reasonable one. Let's start by pointing out the emotions that often lead to success, which I advise against. This is the first:

1st Eagerness or Greed for Power.

Without any doubt, this is one of the feelings where the power of some people who have managed to succeed lies. Normally, as happened with characters like Hitler or Napoleon, they are affected by their triumphs, and they sink in their defeats. Anyway, throughout the history of these characters it clearly shows a feeling of power. Despite being open to criticism, it provides on many occasions situations of provisional triumph.

Inside most of us we possess what some hypocrites call instinct

Gregarious, what psychiatrists call social instinct, and priests call consciousness.

It is the accumulation of feelings such as compassion, gratitude, benevolence, kindness, honor.

It is understood from feelings rooted within ourselves, because the law of life is aware that the human race cannot exceed living in a guild, or striving for survival. These feelings of eagerness, or lust for power, are fought against in a struggle that gives rise to uncertainty, restlessness, restlessness, discomfort, anguish, agitation, pain, anxiety, in an infertile action.

Some human beings have a weak enough social instinct that greed or greed is the primary route, with chances of success. Caligula, and Hitler, went insane.

Do you think it is possible to achieve harmony if you develop your desire, or greed? The very rejection that this idea gives, indicates that it will give you mental problems and incompetence. Only those who are upset can take advantage of this form of triumph.

2º FEAR OF DEFEAT.

This is the second emotion that I do not recommend, despite having been the reason, for some to have achieved the discreet triumph. It has led many people to get a business, or learn a job, to develop legitimate jobs.

However, a fear at a high level cannot remain for a long period of time within a well-furnished head. It can motivate a fleeting job, and temporary, just that.

Heads that are constantly disturbed by fear, thus create the predominant emotion, leading them to

A paralyzing effect.

What's more, a moderate fear will also cause discomfort, lethargy about decision making, denial of events, fear of alterations, disapproval of monotony. The mistakes made in the past, the probabilities of deletions, and the mistakes made today, and in the future, will use your thoughts until you can barely act with enough courage, and bravery, and immerse yourself in a constant situation.

Life has given us fear, as an emotion that well managed can be useful only for emergency situations, when an emergency becomes imminent, in the face of an unexpected escape, or a dangerous event. It is a necessary emotion when a cougar is chasing you, or when you have to avoid a dangerous situation. No one has succeeded out of fear of necessity.

Another way to rate fear is:

Eagerness for Stability

This type of fear is fear itself, but at a lower level, no emotion that has little strength can provide energy. Only a high intensity emotion can provide it. Only a high intensity emotion will bring you success. The laziness of many human beings is the consequence of this type of emotion called the desire for stability, occupying an important place in their work. It is appreciated that antagonistic emotions are normally opposed avoiding this feeling being predominant, and turning it into a reiterative fear of problems.

Some people believe that they are deserved, because their desires are modest, since their main aspiration is not to exceed certain needs, and to obtain stability. The little desire to achieve something of these people, causes a

Compassionate pride, they engage in superior ethical behavior. It is a disappointment since these people without being aware are self-sacrificing. Is your security the only wish you have in this life? How about we render our services to our fellow citizens, not in a meager way, and devoid of fervor, but rather as if we were rendering our services to God. What if we give the best that is within ourselves, without any restrictions, in other words, our commitment to ourselves to serve God, and our fellow men.

The desire for security is similar to fear, to defeat. It is only plausible in an emergency situation. Almost all people who are engaged in low-level commerce hardly keep up with this aptitude. If they have to deal with an emergency, fear arises, they work hard for a short period of time, put their thoughts on fire, until the distressing situation is over.

Later they repeat the same pattern of behavior, worrying about banal aspects, about details of little relevance instead of acquiring a resounding triumph. Luckily for these people, fear is not eternal, they do not have a higher level pattern that motivates their work. Fear, wherever it comes from, has no effect in small proportions, although it carries a risk to logic when it is intense.

3º THE PRIDE.

In third place is pride, this is another of the not recommended emotions as a pattern to follow, to obtain success. Such emotion is often the predominant pattern of people who have achieved a modest, brief triumph. Anger, competition, "the desire that the Martinezes will not surpass me" motivates an important job in a sector of human beings, and this leads them towards a triumph, which in other circumstances would not have been the case.

Nor should pride be completely eliminated. Because it has an added patron advantage. On many occasions, it motivates the athlete in their exercises, the manager of a company that wants to improve the results of their business, compared to the rival company, the opponent of an opposition who wants to get better marks in the exam compared to the rest of your rivals. Underneath the arrogance, there is the motivation that the tireless scientist needs doing tests on his test bench, the lawyer who wants to win a lawsuit, even if his user does not have much money, the doctor who provides his services in a clinic of the social security, where medical attention is free, the worker who performs his performance to the best of his abilities allow him, even if his salary is low, and in rather harsh conditions to carry out.

Pride used as a priority pattern is detrimental. If the job is provisional, such as an athletic competition, a

Competition, competition, etc., can be motivating.

However, in day-to-day work, pride, like the desire for stability, can come back against you, and the other side of the coin is the fear of offense and contempt. Pride, motivated by a challenge, can transform into this same fear, with its headaches, and other mental problems. They become arrogance and, in this situation vexations in the mind are maintained continuously. This disparity and exaltation produce a currency exchange character and a deficiency. Of course, pride is not an emotion that we must develop as a predominant feeling, to instill our progressive progress towards triumph.

THIRD EPISODE.

FOURTH PRECEPT FOR THE TRIUMPH.

For now let us put aside the predominant feelings, which I do not advise, to focus on a feeling that I do advise. In any case, it could be that the readers of this book can make use of this precept as a driver of success, ignoring the rest of the precepts that are detailed in this book, as good or even better than this one.

Despite the fact that this route is one of the most efficient, and is the motivation of many important people, it is difficult for us to develop it, to an intermediate degree, if we are not in possession of certain aptitudes, or innate capacities in our being. This is how I name this route:

4TH AFFECT TO THE WORK.

This does not mean affection for tedious chores, or for the details of little

Relevance, to physical or mental effort. What I am trying to say is the affect that leads to a development, or an elaboration. I mean the affection from which, thanks to it, a work, a task, a creation, a production, etc., arises, I mean by this, that by virtue of the affection towards the task, the most propitious gifts are born for the performance of a task. In many areas it is called an artistic drive. Psychiatrists call it a desire for self-expression, claiming that the vast majority of people have it too.

It is the route that motivates the famous creator, the entrepreneur, sculptor, inventor in all fields, to develop a persevering task. These people are committed to an unbreakable roadmap, since their tasks are carried out with passion, these people live, and believe in what they do. For them there is no obligation to surrender in their performance, since they are flooded with an illusion that gives them a motivation for which to fight in this life. This devotion to the performance of

A task, a management, a task, a commitment, usually motivates entrepreneurs who have succeeded. The very satisfaction that they obtain in the performance of their task, without realizing it removes any negative influence that others may transmit to them. Happiness for the development of a task leads them to success.

It is observed that this stimulus can produce a risk. The person who plunges into this path can lead to instability. The people around you can be affected by a lack of attention to others. He does not tolerate being contradicted and, therefore, runs the risk of having conflicts before the courts, or before society, endangering his hard-earned capital.

With which, although I advise affection towards the task as a complementary route, I do not recommend it as the predominant feeling in the pursuit of victory. It is true that this triumph cannot be achieved without following the

Cited route, but we can look for life looking for an alternative, such as finding a less risky source of enthusiasm. Anyway, most people don't have such a great devotion to doing a job. For this reason you can conserve this important energy source without fear.

The affection to the task, balanced with superior feelings is one of the greatest possibilities of success. Happiness raised to its maximum expression through the performance of a task, designers, writers, are not the only artists. The businessman is an artist in his performance, the manager of a business, the head of a sales section, the coordinator of an event, the director of a company, when he realizes it, and shapes the secrets of life . They love to use their understanding, to produce in their work, not only for financial compensation, but rather, for the affection of the work.

In a company, in a renowned multinational, where employees are mostly mere links in a production chain, it is difficult for the artistic instinct to manifest itself. However, the truth is that those who get the highest level positions, they manage to find one way, or another, to manifest themselves through the performance in their job.

Some supported by emotions of competition, which makes them outperform their production more than the rest of their peers. Others, motivated through a restless mind, learn what it develops in other benefits, and at the same time they do not stop training with courses, seminars, studies, etc., until the day that the management of their company realizes the training this responsible employee with his professional training.

Some other of these workers, who form the links of the great chain of production of

A company does not try so hard to train professionally. Theoretical training manuals do not motivate them to study them, however, they do draw attention to the human designs of people. They are tireless when it comes to communicating with their peers, they know what they think, how they act, they do not lose detail of their virtues, and also their defects, they analyze them in depth. And little by little, they assimilate all the wisdom they acquire from others, which will give them an extra bonus when it comes to exerting their influence over others, gaining leadership, confidence, and prominence in their work environment. The development of this faculty gives them continuous satisfaction, because it is their way of performing. They are trained, like any athlete, for the continuous improvement of their faculties. They get positions above the rest, they become foremen, plant managers, coordinators, section chiefs, etc. They may move to another

Commercial area, reaching positions of certain responsibility. They can influence other merchants, to make payments, or necessary financial investments, to carry out new business purposes, and in which they are rewarded with a new professional promotion.

In the previous paragraph, it is described how many employees have risen from a modest job to a position of greater responsibility. The people who make up this group normally achieve the triumph, because in these people two important feelings appear that act in synergy: Affection for the task, and affection for their peers. These subjects are a faithful reflection, for those people who take into account the precepts that come in the Bible of (serving and loving your neighbor). Having affection for others can be an unconscious emotion. You can imagine that they only care about others out of greed.

No one can imagine within his internal forum, this desire for his fellows, without feeling affection in an unconscious way. These people may never offer anything, although they do. The people around them prefer those who give more than those who are offered.

Mother nature has given these people an innate gift of understanding human nature, skilled at relaxing their internal emotions, when their nerves are on the surface, motivators for expanding development. They get others to trust them. They reap stability among their counterparts, they encourage people to agree on different points of view within a group, they develop an atmosphere of good vibes among co-workers. Their art is composed of subtlety.

Now we are on a route, which I save for another episode: affection for others. It is a higher feeling than affection for the task

For the route of triumph. However, for the moment, we will focus on the last one that has been indicated. Many readers may think that they are positively fond of your work precisely because they use up so many hours of your valuable time. Although the affection for work does not mean in a few words the affection for business, rather affection to manifest the highest level that we possess within ourselves through the work. At the moment that we have to solve great problems, the true affection to the task, does not give rise to allow to leave it in a second place, or to get dizzy by stagnating in monotony.

A successful entrepreneur or farmer can do his job with only a few hours of work a day. In this period of time, these people focus on the most important issues. Including outside the environment of his profession, his mind is focused on these tasks. In this way, you can

Get motivated at any time of the day. In the same way that big businessmen do not tolerate minutiae, or monotony. However, since they have sincere affection for their incessant work, they usually get in a few hours, what other people get in many days of work.

The work of these people is not just a simple escape, rather it is an extension of their most important motivation, the hunch to create, and develop. For this reason, do not question your job for the time it lends you. long hours at work can hide the need for intense discernment.

FOURTH EPISODE.

A FAVORABLE HABIT.

An affection for the job in its proper measure is completely necessary for success. There is another need that I think is even more valuable but, in any case, it has to be united by affection for the task. This other requirement will be discussed in the next episode. Due to this requirement, we will observe that if one cannot feel affection for the task, that it may be feasible to feel affection for the appreciation of a different task. However, in the first instance, it would be advisable to apply a habit, which without being considered necessary, on many occasions is appropriate to obtain affection for the task, up to the level that is necessary to obtain success. It is the habit of:

TREASURE.

I do not advise hoarding just for the sake of it, rather, as a way, to flourish affection for

The work. A constant rise in your bank capital is a palpable indication of economic progress. This progress creates a very powerful hoarding acumen. Without realizing it, he forges routes to facilitate his task, to obtain greater profits, and to treasure more. In this way, their affection for the task is more effective.

An old businessman used to distribute several coins among those closest to him, to instruct them in the habit of hoarding his earnings. For this businessman, this habit was very important, not necessarily because of the few coins that could be collected, but rather, because of the moral support it offers, that impetus for the affection to the task. This is a beautiful thing, aside from the financial gain.

Treasuring financial gains is not possible without emotional support. What is called discipline, no matter how harsh it may be, it will not be possible to turn someone into a hoarder of

Gains from him, unless he has a stimulus. For some people, the fear (hoarding for when times are tough) is enough. However, "it is a jug of cold water, for motivation, the fact of having to constantly walk with a fear of a painful situation," "which risk is for our mental and emotional stability, our entrepreneurial emotion, negotiation, and liberation. "Sometimes it can be convenient, not to be so hoarding. Some people are right to deny this route to hoarding more wealth.

Instead of the pessimistic routes, we must find some positive, in our decision to be hoarders. There is usually a yearning for self-permissiveness. If we do not find a more powerful stimulus, we will not be able to become hoarders. What really drives people to achieve their goals is ambition.

To loosen our desire to squander the

Money, an alternative is to promote our ambition to build our own company, to be owners of a property, a store, a business, what is called active assets, instead of losing our money with passive assets, since the latter Instead of generating wealth, what it does is lose it. However, artists, composers, musicians, inventors, actors, writers, etc., their ambition is that they simply cannot fail to fulfill the objective they have set for themselves, with which, in that situation, either by vocation or conviction , your motivation is more than assured.

Remember that hoarding your savings is just one way to improve your affection for the job. If this hoarding becomes the predominant feeling, and not complementary, the accumulating nature of more and more, it will lead to greed, and in time it could work against you.

FIFTH EPISODE.

AND, FIFTH PRECEPT, FOR THE OBTAINING OF THE TRIUMPH.

Doing a review of, why we comment on the prevailing feelings. It is necessary to insist on this need. First, it was the fourth precept of triumph:

(NOBODY CAN PUSH THEMSELVES TOWARDS SUCCESS; YOU HAVE TO BE DRIVEN BY AN EMOTION OR A DOMINANT, CONSTANT AND LASTING MOOD).

In accordance with this precept, we have understood that someone efficient is someone who is permeated by a feeling, so powerful that other feelings become secondary if we compare it with this predominant feeling, in other words, someone who has the Necessary feelings, so that they act in such a way that they constantly direct you on the same path.

With saying that the qualifiers that are usually used, to indicate efficient, valuable, and competent individuals: we are talking about the vitality that emanates from passion, motivation, enthusiasm, passion, dedication, courage, guts, perseverance, confidence, struggle for constant personal improvement. These terms do not indicate capacities of great intellects, rather mystics. More than a few terms that we may have in mind, they indicate feelings.

It is a question of aptitudes in our personality; the aptitude that originates the predominant good character, and that resides in the person, his constant way of perceiving things. These emotions lead to ideas. The truth is that ideas run the risk of drifting over time, but they usually return to the place of your mind, channeling you down the path that your predominant character establishes. The predominant character of a person is condescension to oneself, the indulgence of some whim, and of the majority

From cravings, he will never conquer.

Continuing with the review, the feelings that lead the individual towards success were also explained, being the following:

1st Eagerness or greed for power.

2nd Fear of defeat.

3º The pride.

4th Affection to the task.

Referring from the first to the third, it is preferable not to be possessed by these feelings. Developing them is not advisable. The fourth feeling is the one that I do recommend, as a predominant emotion. If one is in possession of that emotion, good for you. Most of humanity's talents have it innately. However, the affection towards the task, for the task itself, goes against the human condition.

There are many ways to feel affection for the job, for different reasons. With which, that feeling will be our predominant feeling. What would?. Although there are more feelings with the potential to lead people to success, there are two useful enough to discuss in this book. Being the ones I quote below:

5th Affection for your neighbor.

6. The affection for God.

I can imagine that many of the readers who are reading this book have been stumped. What will God have to do with success? Has he who has triumphed felt affection for his neighbor? I answer these questions that the adjective "affection" has a much deeper meaning than is normally given to it. If puzzled readers want to keep reading to the end of this book, I think most people

You will understand that affection for your neighbor, in its deepest understanding, directs people toward success.

I confirm that the successful entrepreneur serves his neighbor better, because he feels more affection for him. The successful merchant esteems his neighbor to a greater extent than his counterparts, because he continually remains closely with his neighbor. All people understand that in almost all facets of life, the mere fact of being in contact with others is a necessary condition for a person to succeed in life.

However, a person will not find it easy to connect with his peers, if he does not feel affection for them, at least on a certain level. This predisposition towards others, this willingness to remain in contact with others, is affection for other people. It is possible to have a low level, although it is enough with the intention of wanting to provide a service to people to

Derive it into a higher level affection.

The most common type of affection is the servile nature, the desire to get together with others. It is an essential desire of human instinct. If one goes in the opposite direction of this nature, from time to time the injured party becomes withdrawn; someone is born who self-marginalizes, and other psychological pathologies. The aforementioned pathologies are sometimes accompanied by health problems. A withdrawn person is usually unsuccessful, despite sporadic success in some area of his life.

However, I do not incriminate the marginal for not appreciating his peers. It may happen that he esteems them with a good heart, and that he can make pharaonic efforts for others, although his affection is loaded with restrictions, does not manifest itself with full freedom, and does not know how to sow the compensations of this affection. Intuitions, including the servile nature, call for free training and, in the opposite sense, are

It can turn against the person.

This servile nature is exactly the same as the herd instinct. Some people do not have the mental capacity to live alone. In any case, the people who read this book, to a greater or lesser extent, will be people with a concern to improve themselves. Looking in the books for routes to find out why? to this day they have not achieved all that they really want. Investigating different alternatives EXCEPT the correct one: the construction of the capacities that will open the doors for your servile soul to express itself correctly.

In the opposite direction, there will be a few people who read this book, and I comment on it because, this group is within a sector that normally does not sympathize with the study, does not even like to read - for whom the servile nature is a problem. problem, which strikes with his affection towards the task, for the

Route of the servile nature, they try to get out of the mental vicissitudes that the task produces, or of another nature. These people, when they have to develop their work such as public relations, who abducts through the floors of the entrances of discos, hotels, nightclubs, karaoke bars, nightclubs, game rooms, instead of spend enough time to see your users, care about them, their needs, listen to what they have to say, provide what they need within a coherent measure, go in search of potential customers, in order to fill the premises. Although they feel affection for others, this affection is located on a lower rung, and does not direct them towards the powerful feeling of wanting to help others.

SIXTH EPISODE.

A BAD HABIT THAT HAS TO BE AVOIDED.

In the previous episode, we still have not finished explaining the precept number 5, driving force behind the triumph: affection for people. It is very difficult to develop this feeling, to a level that is suitable, if the sincere intention of getting together with our neighbor is not achieved in the first instance. Those who read this book who do not "hang out" easily with others, and to help them in some way, will study deeper aspects of this system later, until we understand how to solve this bad habit of applying too much introspection.

It is an impediment, since it makes it difficult for us to improve ourselves, it is difficult for us to offer our best service to others, if we cannot predominate with whom we relate professionally, and obtain their affection.

Even in a company, it is difficult to advance, if you do not understand how to manage the workers. Regardless of what we do, we must not "impose", we should not have the opportunity to use our faculties efficiently. Starting with a boot polisher, until reaching the president of a very important company, the one he knows how to prevail over others, he achieves whatever he sets his mind to. He who knows how to interact with others, it is possible that he makes a mistake on his way, but there will always be more possibilities to succeed.

In the Bible, we estimate your neighbor, but that will be unworkable, unless we interact with our neighbor, and we come to understand him better. It is not a mere matter of convictions, but rather of efficiency, of a well-established character, and in harmony with the mind. It is our instinct that asks us for this affection to manifest itself through a medium

Constant, and useful, through daily habits,
instead of illusions that navigate the mind of the
withdrawn. To proceed efficiently in most areas,
it is necessary to seek constant understanding
with other people, unless we want to sabotage all
our work effort.

FIFTH LESSON OF THE ECONOMIC
IMPROVEMENT SYSTEM.

Your neighbor will not trust what you offer him,
unless he perceives that you belong to his group,
and gets used to your lifestyle, with its defects
and virtues.

This mistrust caused by a lack of trust, produces
the frustration of many entrepreneurs. Others do
not perceive them as people who belong to their
group. Therefore, it is mistrusted, in other words,
that they are perceived as people who are not
appreciated. People will always feel safe, if the
person with whom they are interacting relates to
them with conviction, and appreciation, it will be
more productive for them, than not having to
relate to the withdrawn. Since the withdrawn
person has problems, to get his benefits
approved, without much help, how valid his
specialty can become.

In our quest to achieve victory, we do not have to act like withdrawn hypocrites, thanking the Messiah, because he has conceived of us differently than others. We must relate to our social environment, it is said with: merchants, carriers, suppliers, manufacturers, etc., listen to their needs, attend to them, they have to see that we care about their concerns in a committed way, if we want to have commercial relationships in the most As fluid as possible, exchanges and transactions have to be done as if you were doing them for yourself, in other words, to your user, mentally speaking, you have to turn it into an extension of your own being, when One works with this conviction, others will perceive in you business complicity, someone in whom they can trust their time, energy, and money.

It may surprise us that at first the reception is somewhat cold. Maybe we haven't

Quite dear to our neighbors, to know how to entertain them, understand them, etc., They perceive us as something "ashy". We hardly know what they think, we know very little about their tasks, and we ignore what is happening around us. Due to our ineptitude, to grasp a variety of clues, which are intrinsic in the existence of those around us, we ignore their sense of humor. We must add that it is also difficult for our neighbors to have to deal with enterprising people like us, just as it is for us to have to deal with them.

In the hypothetical case that our neighbor has to play at home, that advantage will act in their favor, to more easily hide their embarrassment, and appear more qualified towards us, and incidentally, they try to do their part, so that we we feel more comfortable, either by not being too overwhelmed, or by taking care of ourselves more carefully. The embarrassment of him can play a bad

Past, hampering our business relationships. After several disdain, the withdrawn usually reverts to his old habits with comfort. He readily acknowledges that this situation of events cannot be modified. What happens is that his affection for his neighbor is insufficient enough to make the necessary effort. How can we solve this situation, to interact with our neighbors, and be accepted in a commercial environment, to acquire an apprenticeship, and to better provide our services?

Without a doubt, there is no other option, that we will have to do things that we do not like. We are not going to do them either, unless we have a very strong motive. A demonstration would be to resort to our own love. Are we going to throw in the towel, for a difficulty along the way? We can also appeal to our anger by directing it to ourselves, channeling that energy against us.

Inappropriateness.

We can also apply the sixth precept of the economic improvement system, which I will show in an upcoming episode. We know that we should not support ourselves only with the energy of intention, that we have to complement it with a powerful and constant feeling that directs us to carry out cumbersome tasks. Choose between the predominant feelings classified in this book, or from another source of knowledge, but you have to find somewhere, an ENERGY OF PROPULSION. After you have chosen the one that best suits your needs, USE it to endeavor to execute the following plan:

First step, we will go to any area where we have the possibility to communicate with potential partners, and make new contacts. We will take advantage of all the possibilities that our business environment has, so that it expands, and reaches a wider market

Where our service provision can be offered to more users, we will attend conferences, congresses, forums, constantly immersing ourselves in the commercial, business, industrial world, when we find ourselves participating in all these events, it is understandable that we experience as if we were the intruders in a party room. We will endure as long as it takes, to shed the image of a meddler. It is not possible to find and choose partners without first having acquired some qualities, such as public relations. We will appreciate all the possibilities that are presented to us, to exercise these social qualities, for commercial exchanges.

In every business situation we find ourselves in, intention and determination is just as important as presence. Could it be that you don't know how to tell a funny anecdote? There is no reason for you

Do not instruct yourself to know how to take advantage of this, when you witness a positive and happy comment from someone you admire, that situation can be yours, find a time of day, in which you are free from distractions, and Repeat this anecdote mentally as many times as necessary, until it is mentally recorded in your mind, at the same time that you record this anecdote in your unconscious, link this exercise to a kind of calling device, either by touching your ring finger, taking the chin, or any other gesture that does not attract attention, but that at the same time serves you, to resort to this method whenever you need it, in psychology terms it is called an "ANCHOR", the idea is as follows, Whenever you are in some type of commercial event, and the environment is somewhat hostile, you can always use this anchor, and just by touching your ring finger, or any other link that you have chosen, this will serve you well. will go so that automatically

Reproduce this positive anecdote in a good mood, managing to break the ice of any hostile situation, at the same time that you manage to give an image of a person with a Gift of People to your fellow men, over time you will be polishing this skill that will provide you with talent necessary, to get out of austere business situations.

People do not find the approval of commercial exchanges, without having made an effort to dedicate the necessary time. Set aside a portion of your time to acquire a sports habit, no matter if they are disciplines of gentle effort. The world of sport is a type of conversation with many outlets, to which you can always use, to complement your conversations, when it comes to strengthening commercial ties, if we add this to the discipline that is required, to practice a sport with regularly, it will help you to forge a character, so that it is more unbreakable when it comes to

Pursue and achieve your goals.

Now you will tell me: What about academic training? You will not get much of your academic training, if you do not obtain a social skill in the commercial world, for your benefits to be approved, most of the withdrawn would have to spend a couple of years preparing for social practices, and continue to exercise their experience . If this practice is lacking, the people with whom you trade will not approve your business proposals.

Let me get you out of your head, try to socialize with other withdrawn ones, or with people who you think belong to very high-level groups. Since in this situation, he runs the risk of finding himself displaced, inoperative, to start a commercial operation with his counterparts, self-conscious to socialize with others in a favorable way, incapacitated, to offer them the benefit that others

Request: that others feel good with you, this means, not having difficulties when it comes to socializing with you within an atmosphere of cooperation, and exchanges by mutual agreement, where both parties accept the agreed commitments, because they understand that in the end they will come out winning.

At the time when you have executed the previous points, your business contacts will be interested in your services. Previously, if you do not apply esteem to your neighbor, and to socialize with him, you will not support him commercially, which is important to achieve success.

Rather than ignore the servile nature, as many people do, I think it is important to increase esteem. How is it possible to estimate, if the desire to socialize with others is lacking? Honest affection requires strengthening ties, mixing, exchanging ideas and opinions, creating a complicity with those who feel affection. If estimated, you have to

Approve others, with their flaws and virtues.

SEVENTH EPISODE

THE SPIRITUAL MYSTERY OF THE TRIUMPH.

Fear is thought to supply itself for him, and it increases abnormally. The same thing happens with affection. Taking into account that to the first, there is a servile, simple nature, for the affection, the esteem can increase in a high way. It happens the other way around with fear, the affect cannot increase in a distorted way. Affection is the normal situation of the person, the symbiosis that is created between the human being, and all the precepts of God, and of the human condition, it feeds our projects, visualizes our goals and objectives, and achieves the triumph, for our business.

After having given free rein to the servile nature, in order to be able to esteem others with their defects and virtues, what can the next step be? The first step of any

Affection is to make the dear purpose happy. It is understandable that our affection rises, meanwhile, our illusion to make our neighbor happy, reaching the step where we approve all the efforts that are relevant, to achieve this goal.

Our work objective will be our provision of services, giving the best of ourselves, to offer it to our neighbors. Beyond being an obstacle, it has to be a blessing. We can be happy IF WE PROVIDE OUR SERVICES to our neighbor in the best way that we know how to do it, striving for all possible routes, whose purpose is to make our users happy, and the like. In this way we will be channeled towards victory.

In the following paragraph, he encompasses the spiritual mystery of triumph, which he had commented to him at the beginning of this book, being:

LESSON SIX OF THE ECONOMIC IMPROVEMENT SYSTEM.

Exercise your affection for others until your best aspiration is to make them happy. The moment this objective has been consecrated in constant devotion, you will be led towards everything that is vital, to obtain success.

Only those people who honestly give themselves to give the best of themselves, in the provision of their services in full expansion, to a number of subjects that are constantly increasing in number, can aspire to success. This conviction can only come from the affection granted to those who obtain these benefits.

This is the predominant feeling that we seek, therefore, it does not represent any risk to our psychological health, which is in balance with all the precepts

From God, and from human beings, the one that offers us the propulsion we need, for a sustainable utility, and for a value invaded aspirations.

As explained in the previous lessons, we will examine this one, and see if it is approved by the events of the past of humanity, with respect to those who were successful.

Let's examine the following situation, that of two actors. Both play their roles masterfully, both are in possession of the talent, for acting, despite the commentators claiming that they are vulgar actors. With their very normal masteries, neither of them could hope for triumph.

You still have no results. He only acts playing roles that he likes. He wants to win, but does not esteem the public of him. His priority dedication is

Show how good he is by acting. The public feels his cold disposition, and only gives him a simple look. His frustration is complete.

However the following actor, esteems the viewers of him. What he wants most is to make them happy. He plays, the characters that he loves, the audience of him, the way they like him the most. In his eagerness to improve the satisfaction of his audience, he does not stop constantly training, attending acting classes, and drama. He quickly senses if any of his performances are going to downgrade, or upset. He regularly tries to find out with the people with whom he relates, what kind of characters he is to see public. He constantly interacts with his neighbor; first, because he estimates them, then, to know what they want to see. He may go unsuccessful for some time as he struggles to figure out what viewers want, but his morale always remains high.

After a few years of constant training,

Gaining experience, and going through a multitude of castings, with such great affection for achieving his goals that he cannot leave it, the audience begins to accept the affection that the actor dedicates to his viewers. He sees himself as his public, at first he responds with some consideration, then with fervor, and at the end with clamor. As they say: "we have a person like the others; he is with us, he knows what we value, and he values it in the same way. He is attracted to us, in the same way that we are to him. There is a burning of emotions in his interpretations of the films, in which he acts, which is not appreciated with other actors, at least in the cinematographic genre to which he is dedicated ". In no time our actor achieves fame; him getting the win.

However, in the first place, this successful actor did not possess any talent that the other did not possess. He even he possessed fewer qualities than most who do not obtain the

Success, except an enduring affection, which he never decays towards the spectators of him, with which, a predominant feeling, which led him to the great efforts, vital for obtaining success. At this moment we begin to enter the mystery that is hidden, to obtain the triumph that most of the actors in film, television, and theater have. The affection they feel for their audience, they are usually not aware of it.

Many successful actors of different genres will associate the merit of his success with his acting skills, rather than his affection, even though his performances actually leave much to be desired. But they can be forgiven for this arrogance, because they appreciate us. It is not possible for someone who perceives antipathy towards others, or who only feels indifference to others, execute his tasks, or approve of vital efforts, to obtain success in this field.

Comparative precedent can be applied to entrepreneurs, industrialists, merchants, businessmen, investors, executives, manufacturers, shareholders, etc. .

The triumph belongs to that person who feels affection for his users, or clients, giving himself with passion to give the best of himself to these users, to make them happy.

We do not have to think that the affection directed towards human beings can only be exercised through humanitarian works. It can be intensified with lifelong relationships, in the environment of your business, or workplace. The good businessman mixes with the employees of his factory, because these are a link in the chain in charge of raising the company, therefore, the businessman who watches, and cares about his employees, these in turn will strive more, so that the company produces more benefits, producing a symbiosis between the employer and his employees.

In the role that corresponds to it, it develops its affection towards the service it is exercising, and, if it wins, it agrees to seek the appropriate mechanisms, to permanently increase the number of users to whom it provides its services.

There are people who can develop this affection, through mere writing. A prosperous mail-order entrepreneur had the idea to apply it.

I explain how he got it. This entrepreneur focused on reading all the correspondence he received. His competition could use the same tactics as him. What happens is that this businessman is a normal person, from the heap. But he feels empathy for his users, and because they look like him. He has read a great deal of mail, from all the users of his in his long business career; he has sent millions of replies; he has checked how they responded to his mailings,

Being able to get to know his clients a lot, almost like himself. On his advertising posters, his users can interpret that he knows them, and that he feels empathy for them, that he is part of the same group where his clients are. They return his empathy, placing trust in him, they choose him among all the competition. The reason why this result occurs, is an intangible component in the advertising documents, such as the form, procedure, mode, and peculiarity, it is not only the reasoning for the transaction.

I have perceived intangible details, but with a certain difference, in writings of other entrepreneurs about the sale of this same sector. But they do not try to empathize with their customers, by not following the same system of the previous example, with which, the result they obtain is scarce.

What most successful companies have in common is that they understand the

Importance, which has to know what its users want, empathize with them, and focus on satisfying them in order to reach a greater number of customers.

It is obvious that the claim is also financial gain, but many of these entrepreneurs, their spirit of improvement, their entrepreneurial attitude, the challenge of overcoming challenges, makes the path they have to travel to reach their ends, it is as attractive as the financial reward.

I have seen how a street vendor charlatan, at a flea market, would spend some time making a disabled person happy, giving free rein to his ease of speech. He had no reason to do this, except that he enjoyed making this handicap have a good time, just as other people could. This peddler, as he feels an affinity for his neighbor, whenever he has occasion repeats the same role of

Behavior. This does not exempt you from being a charlatan. Whenever the opportunity presents itself, he does not skimp on using his people skills to sell minutiae, at an exaggerated cost.

In any case, if he did not feel an affinity for his neighbor, it would not have been possible for him to acquire this quality of people skills, for street vending. Since his affection never increased enough to want to deal with satisfying his clients, he has only managed to be a mere peddler without pain or glory.

I attest that I, the author of this book, have been the son of vendors from a street stall, in different markets, many years ago, when I accompanied my mother, in a van almost as big as a truck, loaded with all the varieties of gender, that you can imagine, we arrived at the market, at 05:30, in the morning, we took our position, before the others did,

Enduring the harsh cold of winter, and the oppressive heat of summer, I observed my mother as she did the best of herself, in placing all the items she had for sale, in the most exquisite, orderly, methodical way that you Can you imagine, that love that my mother put when exposing all her items to the public, made buyers understand in a subliminal way, the love that my mother felt for her work, the enthusiasm that she put into each sale she made , the sincere gratitude that my mother showed to all her customers, whether they bought her cheap or expensive objects, her dedication when it came to satisfying her customers, was so strong that even if she sold an object of little value, the attention that he dedicated to his client, it was just as intense, as if it were a sale of a very high cost, all the items that my mother sold had been previously reviewed by my father, since my father, mother nature has awarded a Gift , for crafts, and repairs of objects of any

Nature, and nature, but, apart from this, when my father restored any object, he did it with the mental conviction that in the end it was going to be for him, therefore, my mother every time she sold an item, she was so reliable as if it were new, everything he sold was of high quality, to all this, we must add the sympathy and affection he showed to each of his customers, over time I realized that most of their customers returned to buy more items, because they knew that buying from my mother was a guarantee of quality, the word spread about the different trinkets, where we came from, therefore, our clientele rose week after week, and with the Hand on my heart, I can guarantee you that my parents before retiring from their market stall, were the ones who sold the most compared to their neighbors, and another thing no less important, they were also the most loved, and appreciated by the majority of the users, who visited the market. This experience that I lived with my

Parents, it has remained within me, throughout this time, and now I share it with all of you, because the example that my parents have given me, of always doing the right thing, with effort, passion, and affection, or later, Or earlier, in the end the success ends up coming.

The affection of a person has to increase, he has to be transmuted into a true passion, to take care of himself in the best possible way as explained in the sixth lesson, before waiting for a great triumph. The affection for others must be so immense that it must naturally motivate the desire to help, just as the doctor does to his patients.

Most of the successes entail an effort, and a very great sacrifice, only viable, for those who are possessed by a powerful feeling, and lasting in time. At the moment in which these people manifest, that (they choose the procedures before the results), they indicate an affection towards their

Neighbor, and a longing to help him, and it would be even more respectable, if done unconsciously. Many people practice more people, providing their services in a more positive way, than those who do it in an interested way, and fully aware of it. Pay attention to this beautiful precept collected from the Bible:

"Serve from the heart, as obeying the Lord and not men."

It is the first reason in this transaction of benefit by benefit, which makes coexistence viable. Day-to-day necessities, nourish the hungry, hydrate the thirsty, house the homeless, make people happy with a large number of benefits. These people are the best architects of all the people who provide their services.

EIGHTH EPISODE.

SIXTH PRECEPT OF THE ECONOMIC
IMPROVEMENT SYSTEM.

In the previous episodes, we have analyzed all
the most convenient overriding feelings, to
provide you with the "boost" that is needed for
success, except one. Some have shortcomings,
others are useful to twenty percent of people.
There is a prevailing sentiment without risk,
which can be used by all people who are
interested in religion. It consists of affection for
God. On the assumption that you do not have
any religion, your best card is "affection for
others", although if you are linked to a religion,
your "affection for God" can be very efficient, if
you understand joining the " spiritual devotion
"with the rendering of his daily services.

We understand that a distributed loyalty can tear
the human being, it is possible that it causes a
mental struggle, that destroys any

Efficiency. Just as a distributed allegiance can fragment a person, an exclusive allegiance can offer him, without any doubt, heavenly vigor and power. This happened to Nelson Mandela. We have to dedicate ourselves entirely to loyalty, to find the route that leads us to a life formed of full motivation, and of true success.

This conviction will give you great power. Laziness, mental problems, which hinder its efficiency, will be eradicated. At this moment, you are a PERSON WITH A GOAL. All feelings are bent, to attend the great feeling. A balance is born, which facilitates the power of a well-balanced attitude. The transit of its ascent becomes so majestic, like that of an ocean.

Being motivated by affection towards God, is one of the straightest paths to success, motivates to execute the greatest sacrifices, is the promoter of the most beautiful achievements, and offers the

Most pleasant bliss.

NINTH EPISODE.

THE PROJECT TO REACH YOUR OBJECTIVE.

The spiritual recipe of the economic improvement system is in front of you. In order to be successful, be happy to have the opportunity to apply the episodes described here, plan a roadmap, which is based on the information detailed here, and whatever happens, move on.

Read this system as many times as you see fit, and use it again when you need to remember it, and incidentally, it will give you a boost of motivation. Following it is the most complicated, as is the case with most systems, but I have designed some add-ons, which could facilitate your dedication, in the first place, it will be to be able to maintain permanent motivation.

Most people who read this book will know how to make a roadmap. Others

They may at this point have certain discrepancies with what is exposed here, with which, they will not be very much for the work, of making their own plan, unless things are made easier for them in this regard. It is also possible that there is another group of readers, who choose to apply only a portion of the information found in this book, however, acting in this way, they are already beginning to develop an action system, which is what I want, adapted to your particular needs, or, also if possible, the case of adapting it to your own character, and individual psychology, and therefore, more specific when it comes to meeting your individual needs.

The route to follow that I now indicate is by way of recommendation. Take something to write with, and as you understand what I convey to you, adapt each section, in order to adjust it to your own needs and individual capabilities. As soon as it is finished, you will be able to check the result of your own

Roadmap, from which you will have the necessary support, to obtain the success you want so much.

SECTION ONE.

If you are not lending your work to a user yet, now is the time to start.

Most of the people who obtain financial compensation, either because they provide their services in a temporary, permanent, liberal job position, in the business world or, of any other nature, are already offering a benefit to the public, with which, it is justified to study this first section. Now we focus especially on the unemployed, the person who is looking for a job, or those who are still training academically. In this circumstance, is it possible to provide any service? sure yes, and in different ways.

1º.- Choosing the type of benefit, where a better activity can be offered. (It can

Consult the Internet pages, to find a multitude of services, in a large capital, that perhaps, you have never heard, but at the same time, you are able to carry out this type of task).

2º.- Training, to carry out this type of activities efficiently.

3º.- Instructing oneself to meet people, thanks to the habit acquired from a servile nature, to learn how to make our clients happy.

4th.- Exercising in the practice of conversation, with the gift of people, in any area of our lives, either, interacting with a neighbor, classmate, with a co-worker, user, client, supplier, etc. ., since the main objective is that all our users remain completely satisfied with the service we offer, and that transaction always begins with fluid communication, and

Harmonious.

5º.- Carrying out our work in a constant way, for example: as spokesperson of a forum, delegate of an assembly, representative of a group, coordinator of a group, member of a union, member of an organization. The idea is to get into the habit, to start being part of this society that we have had to live in, and once this base is fostered, start with a provision of our services, in exchange for financial compensation.

6º.- Expanding to new horizons, that is, starting from the base of section number 5, do not skimp on the possibility of joining with other groups, which are outside of which you already belong, since acting in this way, it will provide an extra push, in order to find more opportunities for commercial exchanges, which is what you ultimately want.

7º.- Get used to dealing with people who in a

Future will become your users, interact with them, since by acting in this way, you will get to know them better, and thus you will know how to serve them in the best possible way.

8º.- Cooperate with your neighbor, since by acting in this way, you get your neighbor to consider you as one of their own, and this is a fundamental pillar, to gain the trust of others, since without trust, your Future client, or user, will not trust enough, to make commercial exchanges, in the future with you.

SECOND SECTION.

1º.- In the event that you already have a job, a business, a store, bar, restaurant, hotel, company, industry, etc., try to improve your services, analyzing what your customers demand, and Once this information is obtained, try to adapt your services to the needs of your clients, and do not skimp on satisfying them, since whoever takes care of their

Clients, it's like taking care of yourself.

2º.- Adapt the information that is detailed in this book, to all your singularities with respect to your current situation, to get the most out of this system.

SECTION THREE.

Develop a predominant, vigorous, constant, plausible feeling that directs you permanently towards your goal, accepting the efforts that this entails, without stopping on your way until you reach the goal.

If this motivation of drive is lacking, the first section, and second, like all the others, will be like the requests that are made at the beginning of a new year: the first is faced with great enthusiasm, but as the year, they fade away as a mere memory.

Bearing in mind envy, revenge, and other feelings, which if used can

Achieve some type of result, although personally, I do not recommend them, but the few precepts that promote success that have some consideration are the ones that I quote below:

FIRST.- Eagerness for power.

SECOND.- Fear of defeat.

THIRD.- Pride.

FOURTH.- Affection to the task.

FIFTH.- Affection for others.

SIXTH.- Affection for God.

Do not choose any until you have first assessed all the risks that have been explained in the previous lessons. I advise precept number 4, but it has its dangers. I wholeheartedly advise precepts number 5, and 6, since these are without any risk. I recommend that you focus on the last three precepts, making them your main asset,

To obtain the triumph.

Many of the people who read this book, feeling identified with the realism of things, will choose the fourth precept. When they experience various penalties that arise, when maintaining this precept, they will choose the fifth precept. Since it is easier to feel affection for the task, if you also feel affection for your neighbor, to whom you provide a service. The sixth precept is the wisest choice, Bearing in mind that people are not perfect beings, it is difficult to continue feeling affection for others, without the enthusiasm that God transmits to us.

FOURTH SECTION.

"Find a way to improve your stamina each time you decline."

Try to find this medium, through self-help books, magazines, specialized Internet pages, seminars, etc., until you find

That methodology, which is adapted to your specific needs, getting the best out of you, so that in this way you are prepared, when it comes to preventing the moment that the first symptoms of discouragement appear, and that under no circumstances can discourage you in your career to achieve your success.

FIFTH SECTION.

If your motivation continues to wither, see if you are on the right track, according to your claims, to achieve what you really want. If not, find another goal that gives you that extra motivation you need to achieve your goals.

SECTION SIX.

When you have obtained a high-level position, due to your business, commerce, company, etc., choose the people who can transmit your knowledge to them, and at the same time, you never give up to continue acquiring more

Knowledge, wherever it comes from, even the most humble employee of your company, at any given time, you can give a whole lesson, remember: "information is power", incidentally, do justice to the employees who work for You, ascending those who have shown signs of personal improvement, and who have shown a sincere concern to do everything necessary to raise your company, remember that the employer who looks after his employees is the one who also looks after his company, position that employees are a very important link in the chain, charged with leading a company to success.

Spend time and energy on advertising marketing, as this area is responsible for making your products known to more people, and therefore to potential new consumers of your services. Remember, the one who is successful is the one who focuses on a group

Of clients, whose number is constantly expanding, instead of focusing on a reduced audience of consumers, with which, having an advertising endorsement is essential.

SEVENTH SECTION.

This is advice focused on domestic savings, taking into account that an active asset is anyone who generates money, such as: someone who rents a home, sets up a business, a factory, etc., and a passive asset is The one that apart from not producing any economic benefit, after its acquisition suffers a devaluation over time, such as the purchase of a motorcycle, car, jewelry, etc., my advice is, that you try to acquire more active assets, that not passive, since by acting in this way, you always make sure of having an economic surplus in your life, with this I do not mean that you have to have an austere life, since if you sacrifice yourself in this life, it is logical what

I would like to have in return, a compensation that justifies so much effort, but I do want to say that you can indulge yourself from time to time, so that your mental health obtains a reward after the effort, without all of them being ruined. Your profits.

And now I can only say that I wish you with all my heart that you achieve everything you set out to do, that you obtain success, triumph, and much happiness in your lives.

The fact of feeling love for your work, for your neighbor, and for God, that is a quality that honors you, but in your quest to acquire wisdom, above all you have to learn "to swim, and put your clothes away", because never you must lower your guard, since there is outside is full of wolves. JESUS CHRIST SAID: The work I send you to do is dangerous. It is like sending sheep to a place full of wolves. So be smart and attentive like snakes, but also be humble, like doves. (Matthew 10:16)